W9-AAX-489

The Science of Sound Waves

Robin Johnson

Crabtree Publishing Company
www.crabtreebooks.com

Crabtree Publishing Company

www.crabtreebooks.com

Author: Robin Johnson

Series research and development: Reagan Miller

Editorial director: Kathy Middleton

Editor: Janine Deschenes

Proofreaders: Ellen Rodger and Petrice Custance

Design: Ken Wright

Cover design: Ken Wright

Photo research: Ken Wright, Robin Johnson

Production coordinator and Prepress technician: Ken Wright

Print coordinator: Margaret Amy Salter

Animation and digital resources produced for Crabtree Publishing by Plug-In Media

Photo Credits:
Thinkstock: p4 (boy); p11; p13 (top); p14; p19

All other images from Shutterstock

Library and Archives Canada Cataloguing in Publication

Johnson, Robin (Robin R.), author
The science of sound waves / Robin Johnson.

Includes index.
(Catch a wave)
Issued in print and electronic formats.
ISBN 978-0-7787-2941-9 (hardcover).--
ISBN 978-0-7787-2966-2 (softcover).--
ISBN 978-1-4271-1855-4 (HTML)

1. Sound-waves--Juvenile literature. I. Title.

QC243.2.J638 2017 j534 C2016-907052-2
C2016-907053-0

Library of Congress Cataloging-in-Publication Data

Names: Johnson, Robin (Robin R.)
Title: The science of sound waves / Robin Johnson.
Description: New York, NY : Crabtree Publishing Company, 2017. | Series: Catch a wave | Audience: Age 8-11. | Audience: Grade 4 to 6. | Includes index.
Identifiers: LCCN 2016051655 (print) | LCCN 2016051948 (ebook) | ISBN 9780778729419 (reinforced library binding : alk. paper) | ISBN 9780778729662 (pbk. : alk. paper) | ISBN 9781427118554 (Electronic HTML)
Subjects: LCSH: Sound-waves--Juvenile literature.
Classification: LCC QC243.2 .J644 2017 (print) | LCC QC243.2 (ebook) | DDC 534/.2--dc23
LC record available at https://lccn.loc.gov/2016051655

Crabtree Publishing Company
www.crabtreebooks.com 1-800-387-7650

Printed in Canada/032017/BF20170111

Published in Canada
Crabtree Publishing
616 Welland Ave.
St. Catharines, Ontario
L2M 5V6

Published in the United States
Crabtree Publishing
PMB 59051
350 Fifth Avenue, 59th Floor
New York, New York 10118

Published in the United Kingdom
Crabtree Publishing
Maritime House
Basin Road North, Hove
BN41 1WR

Published in Australia
Crabtree Publishing
3 Charles Street
Coburg North
VIC, 3058

CONTENTS

Hi, I'm Ava and this is Finn. Welcome to the world of waves! In this book you will learn all about sound waves – from their common properties to the ways they travel through different mediums.

After reading this book, join us online at Crabtree Plus to learn more about wave patterns, types, and uses! Just use the Digital Code on page 23 in this book.

SOUNDS ALL AROUND

Have you heard about sound? It is all around you! Your alarm clock rings and jolts you out of bed in the morning. The toaster dings and up pops your breakfast. A loud bell calls you to school and later sends you home again. Your parrot squawks, a horn honks, your smartphone buzzes, and your music plays until it is time for bed. You hear all sorts of sounds from morning to night, but what is sound?

SOUND IS ENERGY

Sound is a form of **energy**. Energy is the power to do work. There are many other forms of energy on Earth. Light is a form of energy that you can see. Heat is a form of energy that you can feel. Sound is energy that you can hear with your ears.

SHARING INFORMATION

Sounds help us send and receive messages. The wail of a siren tells us a fire truck is on the way. The whistle of a kettle tells us it is time for hot cocoa. Sounds also help us communicate. When people **communicate**, they share ideas and information. People communicate in all sorts of ways with spoken words. They share stories, whisper secrets, and sing songs.

WHAT DO YOU THINK?

Think of all the sounds you hear each day. What information do they give you? How do you use sounds to communicate with others?

WITHOUT A WORD

People also communicate without using any words at all! You might sigh and tap your fingers when you are bored. You might whistle when it is time for recess and groan when you get homework. We can **interpret** the sounds people make to get information about them. To interpret means to understand the meaning behind an action, mood, or behavior.

WHAT IS THE MATTER?

There are sounds all around you. But did you know that there is **matter** all around you, too? Matter is anything that takes up space and has **mass**. Mass is the amount of material in an object. There are some types of matter you can see. Hamsters, running shoes, and milk are matter you can see. There are other types of matter, such as air, that you cannot see. Air is a **gas**.

All of these things are made of matter.

This is a tuning fork. It vibrates when it is hit and makes a sound.

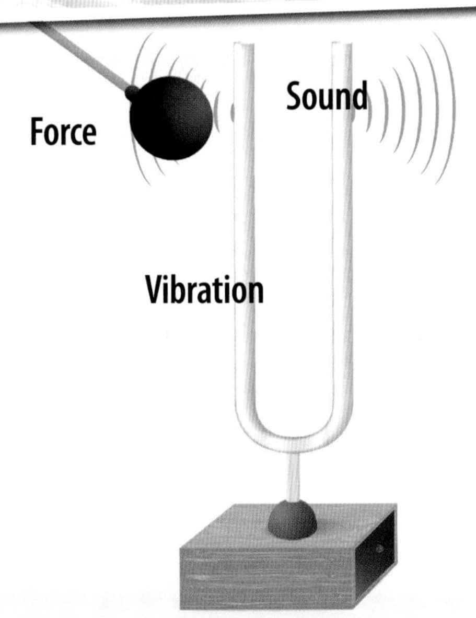

A MOVING MATTER

Sounds are produced when matter **vibrates**. To vibrate means to shake or move back and forth with very short, quick movements. Matter vibrates when a **force** is applied to it. A force is a push or pull that can make an object move. When the object vibrates, it produces the sound energy that we hear.

TO SEE OR NOT TO SEE

Sometimes you can see matter vibrate and produce sound. When you pluck a guitar string, the force of your finger makes the string move quickly. You can see the string vibrate. You can hear the sound of the music that the guitar makes. When you use an electric toothbrush, you can see and feel it vibrating in your hand. You hear the buzzing sound that it makes.

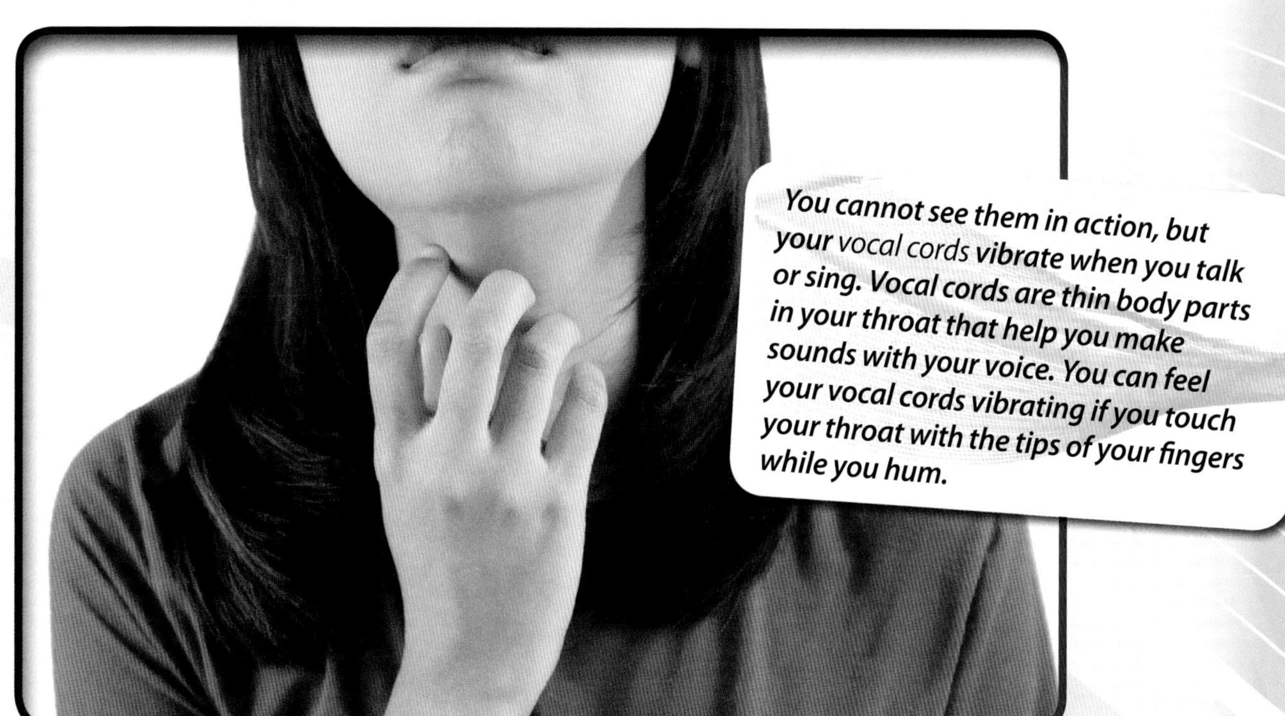

You cannot see them in action, but your vocal cords *vibrate when you talk or sing. Vocal cords are thin body parts in your throat that help you make sounds with your voice. You can feel your vocal cords vibrating if you touch your throat with the tips of your fingers while you hum.*

TOO SMALL TO SEE

Usually you cannot see matter vibrate. That's because the **vibrations** are too small to see. When you shoot a hockey puck, the force of your shot makes the puck vibrate. You cannot see the vibrations, but you can hear the sound when your stick hits the puck. When you open a jar of jam, you cannot see the lid vibrating. But you can hear the sound energy that it produces. If you dropped the jar, that would make a vibration too. You would hear a crash and find yourself in quite a jam!

FROM THE SOURCE

All sounds come from a **source**. The source of a sound is the person or thing that produces a vibration. When you watch television, the TV is the source of the sound. When you fight with your brother over the remote, you are both sources of sound. When your mother gets mad and turns off the TV, it is no longer a source of sound!

WHAT DO YOU THINK?

Name the sources of sound that you see in this picture. Can you see the sound waves that they produce? Explain why or why not.

NEAR OR FAR

Sometimes you are near the source of a sound. You are close to your best friend when they whisper a secret in your ear. Other times, you are far from the source of a sound. The phone rings in the kitchen and you can hear it upstairs. A siren wails and you can hear it from many blocks away. Whether you are close to a sound or far from it, it must travel some distance for you to hear it. You can hear sounds because energy travels from the source to your ears. But how does sound move?

SOUND WAVES

Sound travels in **waves**. Waves are regular **patterns** of motion. A pattern is something that repeats. You cannot see sound waves, but they are all around you. They spread out from the source of a sound in all directions. If you could see sound waves, they would look like ripples of water in a pond after you throw in a stone.

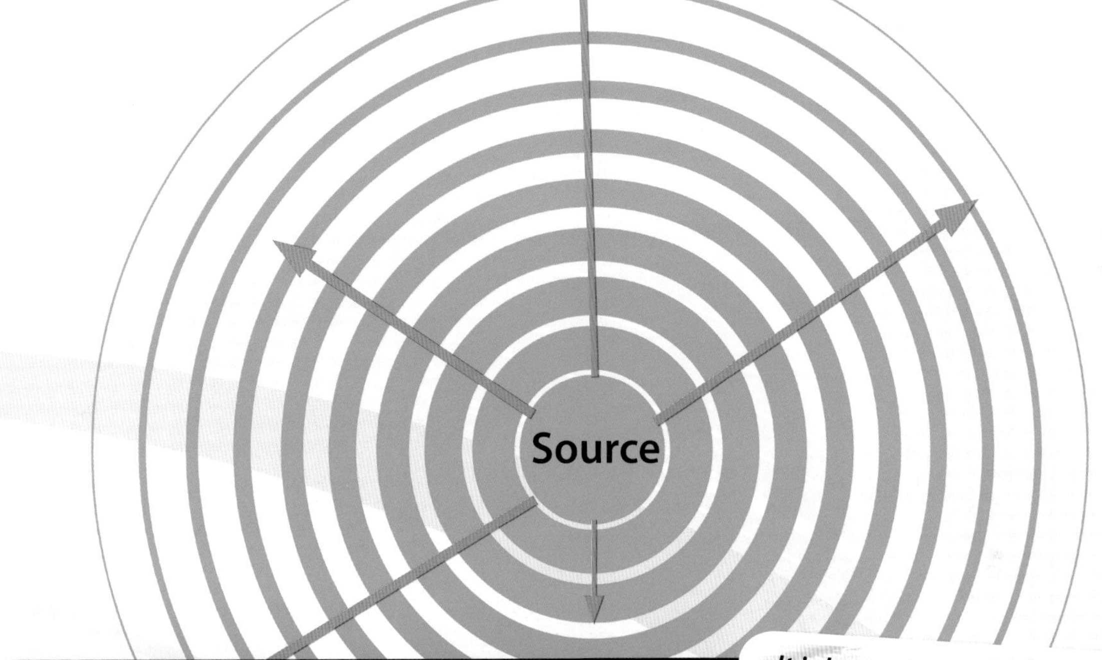

It is hard to hear someone talking on a very windy day because some of the sound waves get blown away!

CARRYING SOUNDS

Sound waves need a **medium** to travel. A medium is any matter that carries waves of energy. There are three forms of matter—gas, liquid, and solid. Most of the sounds you hear travel through air, which is a type of gas. Sound can also travel through water and other liquids. It can even travel through wood, bricks, and other solids. If sound did not travel through solids, you would not hear birds chirping in trees and cars honking when you are inside your home.

PIECES OF MATTER

All matter is made up of **molecules**. Molecules are very tiny pieces of matter. When the source of a sound produces a vibration, it causes the molecules beside it to vibrate. The vibration of these molecules causes the molecules around them to vibrate, too. The molecules keep vibrating, transferring energy from one molecule to the next. The vibration of the molecules carries sound through a medium and to our ears.

WAVE GOODBYE

Sound waves can travel through mediums, but they cannot keep going forever. As they move farther away from the source of the sound, sound waves run out of energy. The sound waves get weaker and weaker until they no longer have enough energy to make molecules vibrate. Then the sound stops.

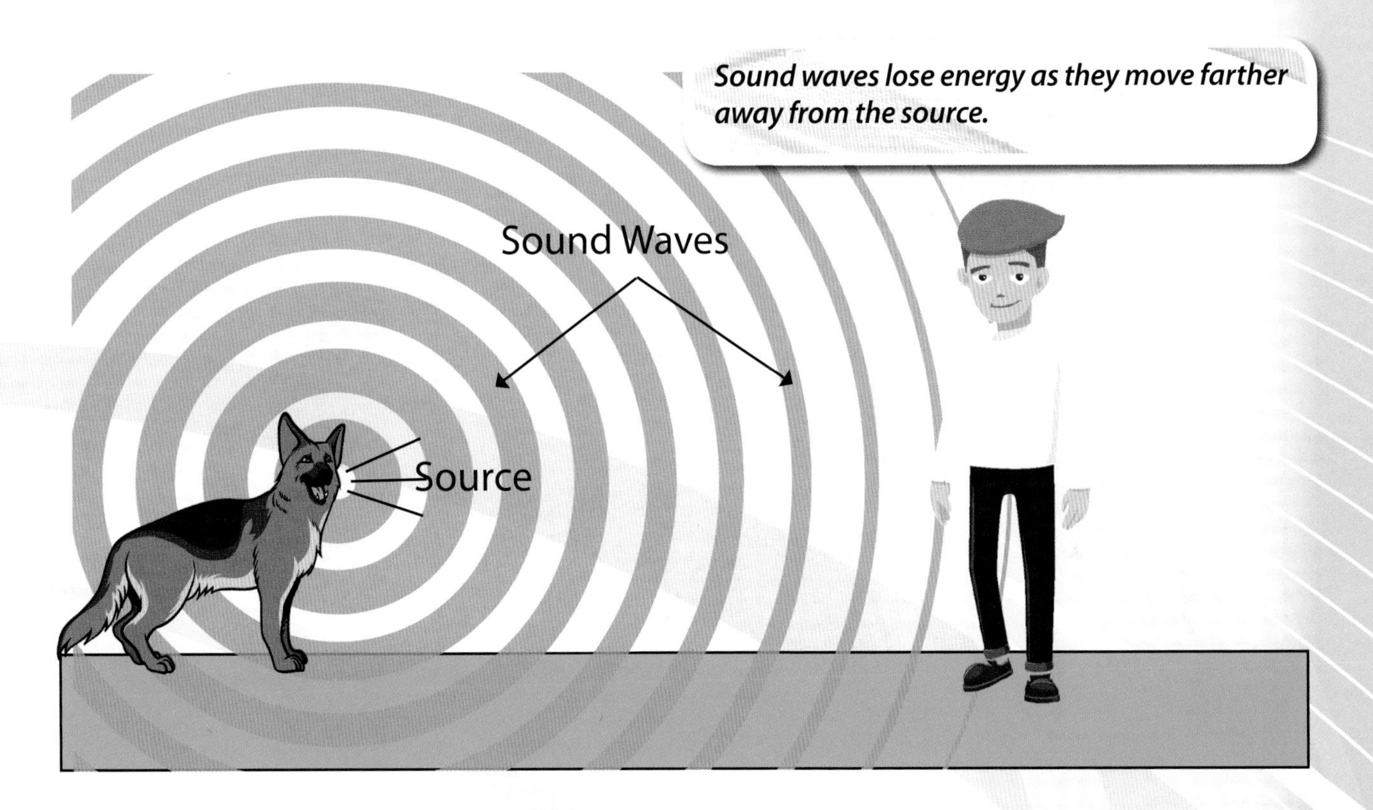

Sound waves lose energy as they move farther away from the source.

STOP THAT NOISE!

If sound waves did not run out of energy, we would keep hearing the same sounds over and over again. A dog would bark, and we would hear the bark again and again. The dog's bark would be worse than its bite! A phone would ring, we would answer it, and then it would keep ringing! If sound waves never stopped, our world would be very confusing—and very noisy!

OFF THE WALL

Sound waves can travel through matter, but they can also be **reflected** off it. To reflect means to bounce off something. When sound waves strike a wall, door, or other hard object, sound is reflected back toward the source of the sound. Sometimes you can hear these reflected sound waves as echoes. You can hear echoes in small spaces with hard walls, such as tunnels and wells. You can also hear **echoes** in large places that have hard surfaces all around them. For example, if you yell into a big, rocky canyon, your voice will come back to you as an echo.

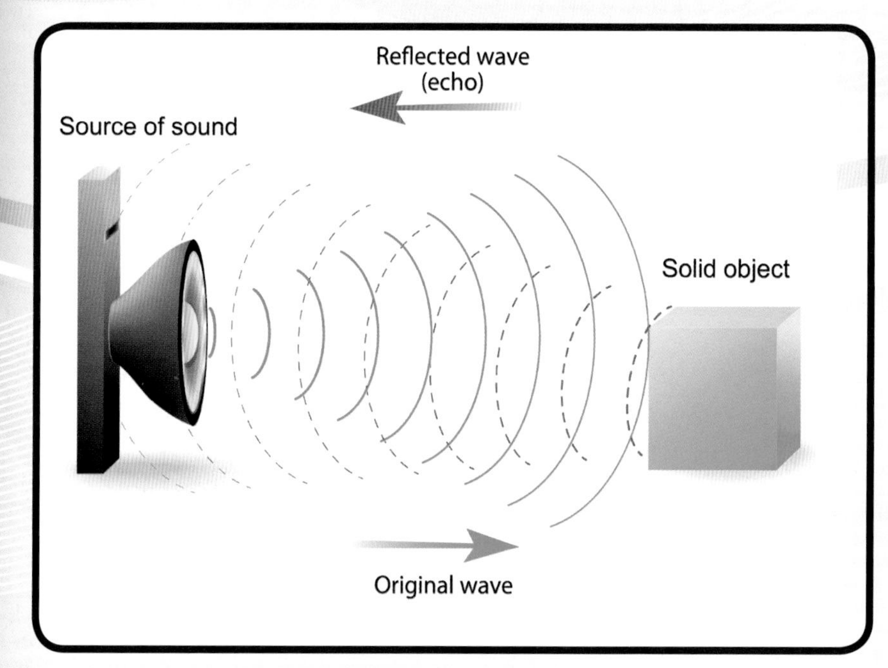

USING ECHOES

Some animals use echoes to travel and find food at night or in dark places. For example, bats make clicking sounds with their mouths. The sound waves hit trees, insects, and other objects and bounce back to the bats. The bats use the echoes to figure out the size, shape, and location of the objects. Using echoes to locate things is called **echolocation**.

SOAKING UP SOUND

Sound waves can also be **absorbed** by matter. To absorb means to soak up. Soft materials, such as chairs, pillows, and curtains, soak up the energy in sound waves. Without energy, the sound waves cannot travel any farther and the sound stops. People use soft materials such as carpets to absorb some of the sounds in their homes. Without them, sound would bounce and echo loudly around the rooms.

Luckily, the couch, pillows, and blankets absorb some of the sounds at this sleepover!

HEAR! HEAR!

Have you heard how you hear? Your ears catch sound waves as they travel from place to place. The human ear is made up of three main parts—the outer ear, the middle ear, and the inner ear. The outer ear traps sound waves as they pass by. The outer ear is the part of the ear you can see. It acts as a funnel to collect sound and direct it into the middle ear.

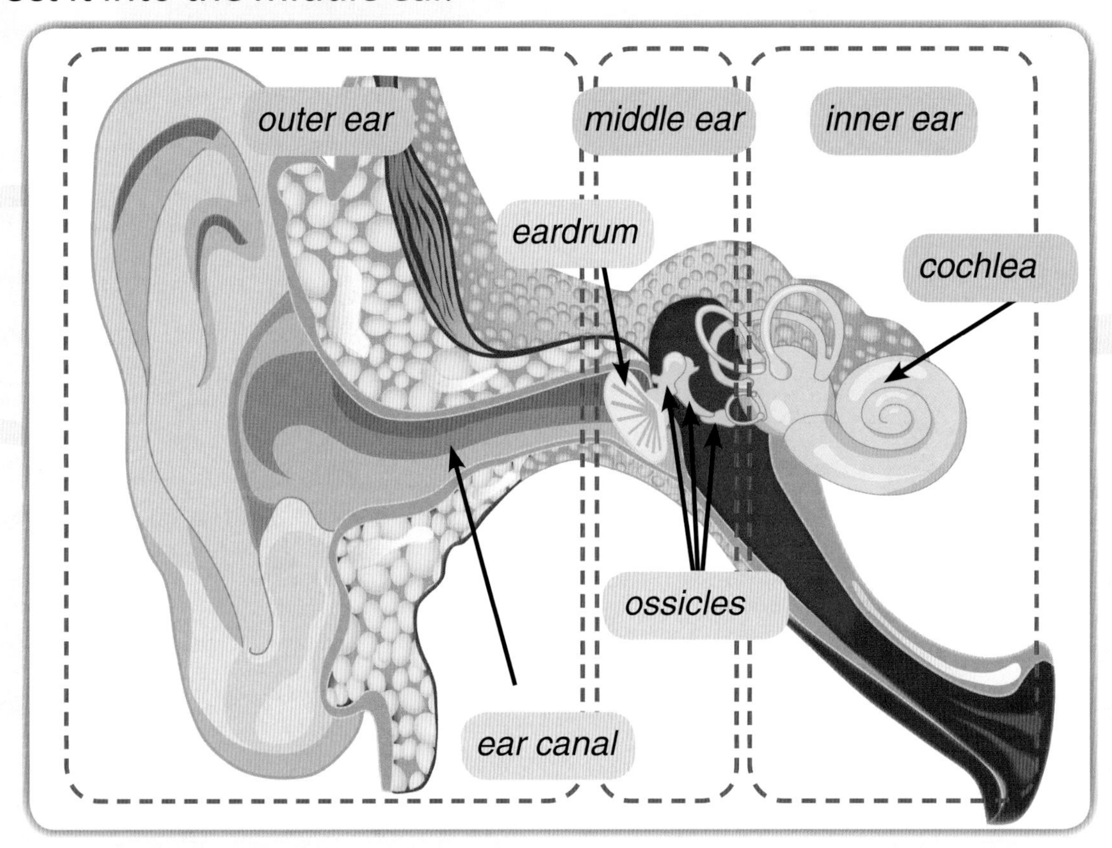

THE MIDDLE EAR

Once sound waves enter your ear, they travel along a tube called the **ear canal**. Then the waves reach the **eardrum** in the middle ear. The eardrum is a thin piece of skin that is stretched tightly like a drum. The eardrum vibrates when sound waves hit it. The vibrations of the eardrum cause the **ossicles** to move back and forth. The ossicles are a set of three tiny bones that are linked together. They are the smallest bones in the human body, but they do a big job. When the ossicles vibrate, they help move sound from the middle ear to the inner ear.

THE INNER EAR

Sound waves enter the inner ear through a small, snail-shaped tube called the **cochlea**. The cochlea is filled with liquid and lined with thousands of tiny hairs. The hairs vibrate and send signals to the brain. The brain makes sense of these signals and interprets them as different sounds.

Some animals have large ears for catching sounds. Rabbits use their big ears to help them avoid danger.

You can cup your hand behind your ear to catch more sound waves and funnel them into your ear. People sometimes do this when they want to hear something better.

ALL SORTS OF SOUNDS

Your ears catch all sorts of sounds. Some sounds are high and squeaky, while others are low and rumbly. Some sounds are so loud that you cover your ears to block the noise. Other sounds are so soft that you are not sure you heard them at all. What makes all the sounds you hear so different?

*Amplitude is measured from the center of the wave to its **crest** or **trough**.*

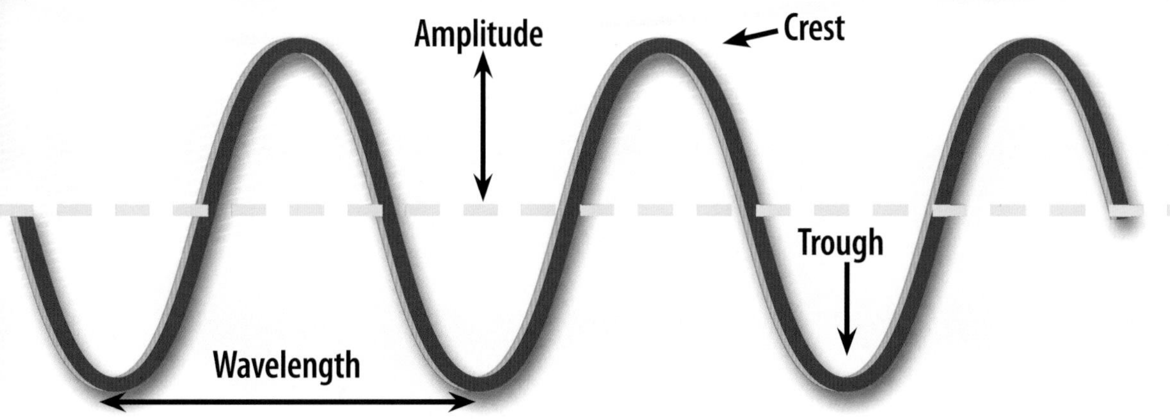

HEIGHT AND LENGTH

Sound waves have many different properties. **Amplitude** is the height of a wave. Sound waves can have high or low amplitudes. **Wavelength** is the distance between any two peaks of a wave, called crests, or any two low points of a wave, called troughs. Some wavelengths are short and others are long.

JUST PASSING BY

Frequency is another property of sound waves. Frequency is how often waves pass in a set amount of time. A sound wave can have a high or low frequency, depending on the amplitude and wavelength of the wave. The diagrams below show sound waves with different frequencies.

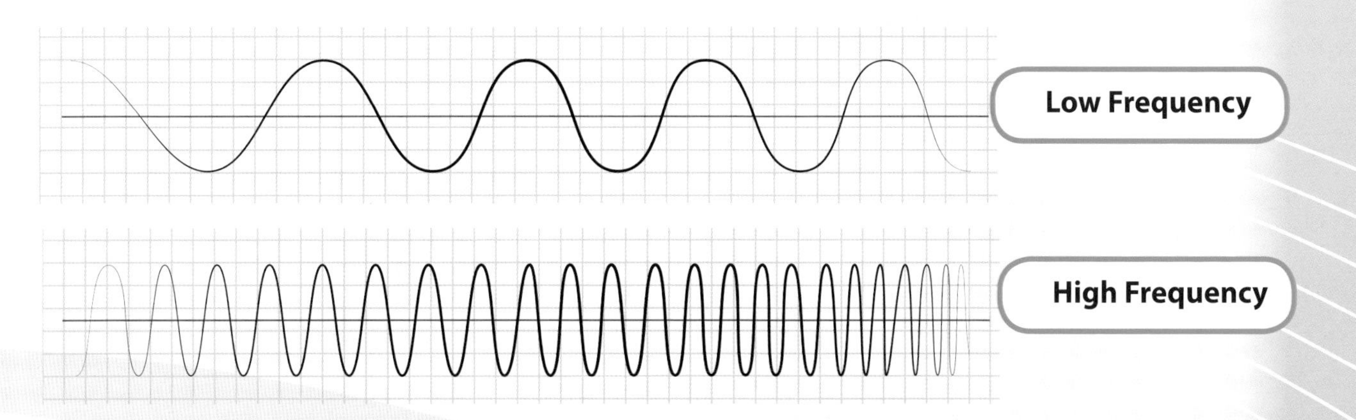

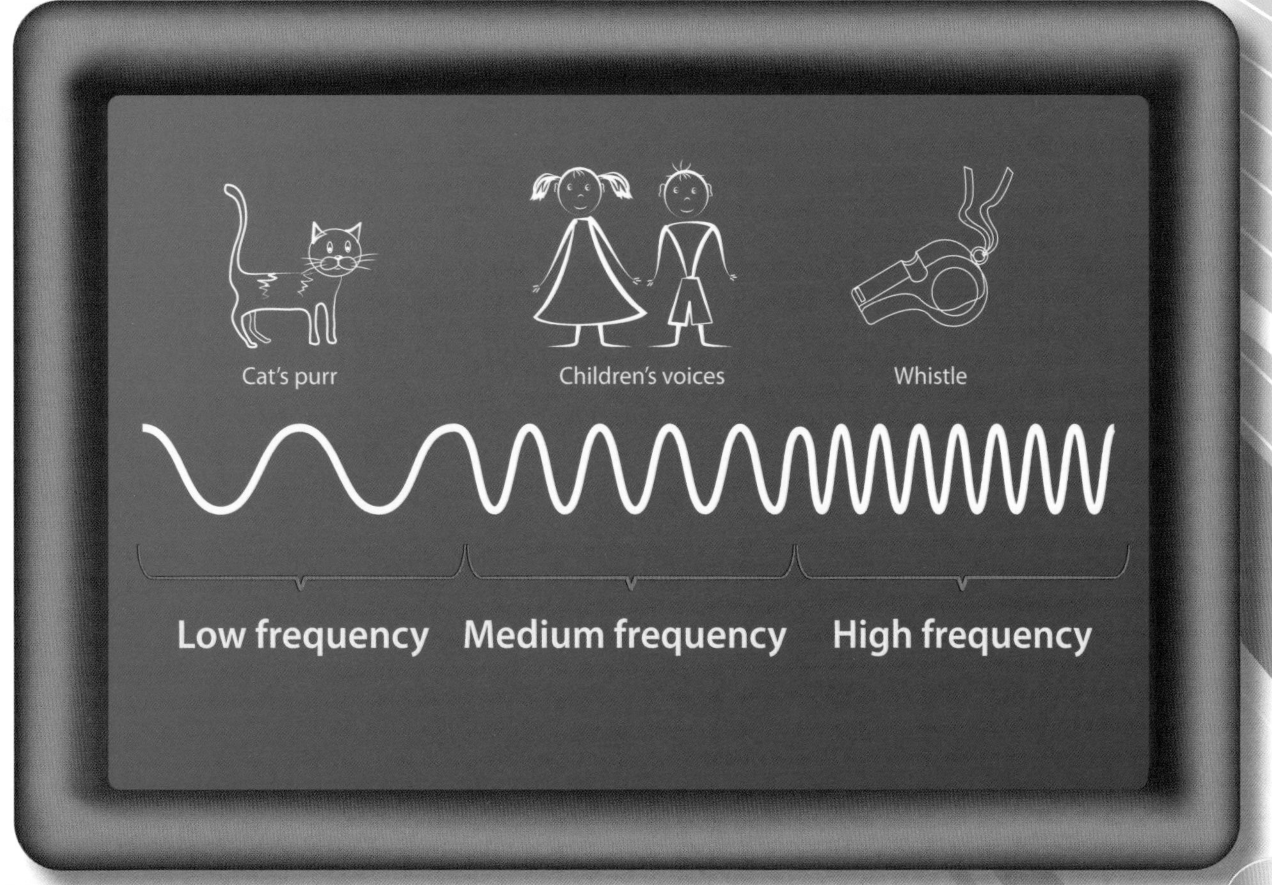

PITCH PERFECT

The frequency of a sound wave tells us how fast the wave is vibrating. A high frequency means a sound wave has a short wavelength and is vibrating quickly. A low frequency means a sound wave has a long wavelength and is vibrating slowly. We hear these differences in frequency and wavelength as **pitch**. Pitch is how high or low a sound is.

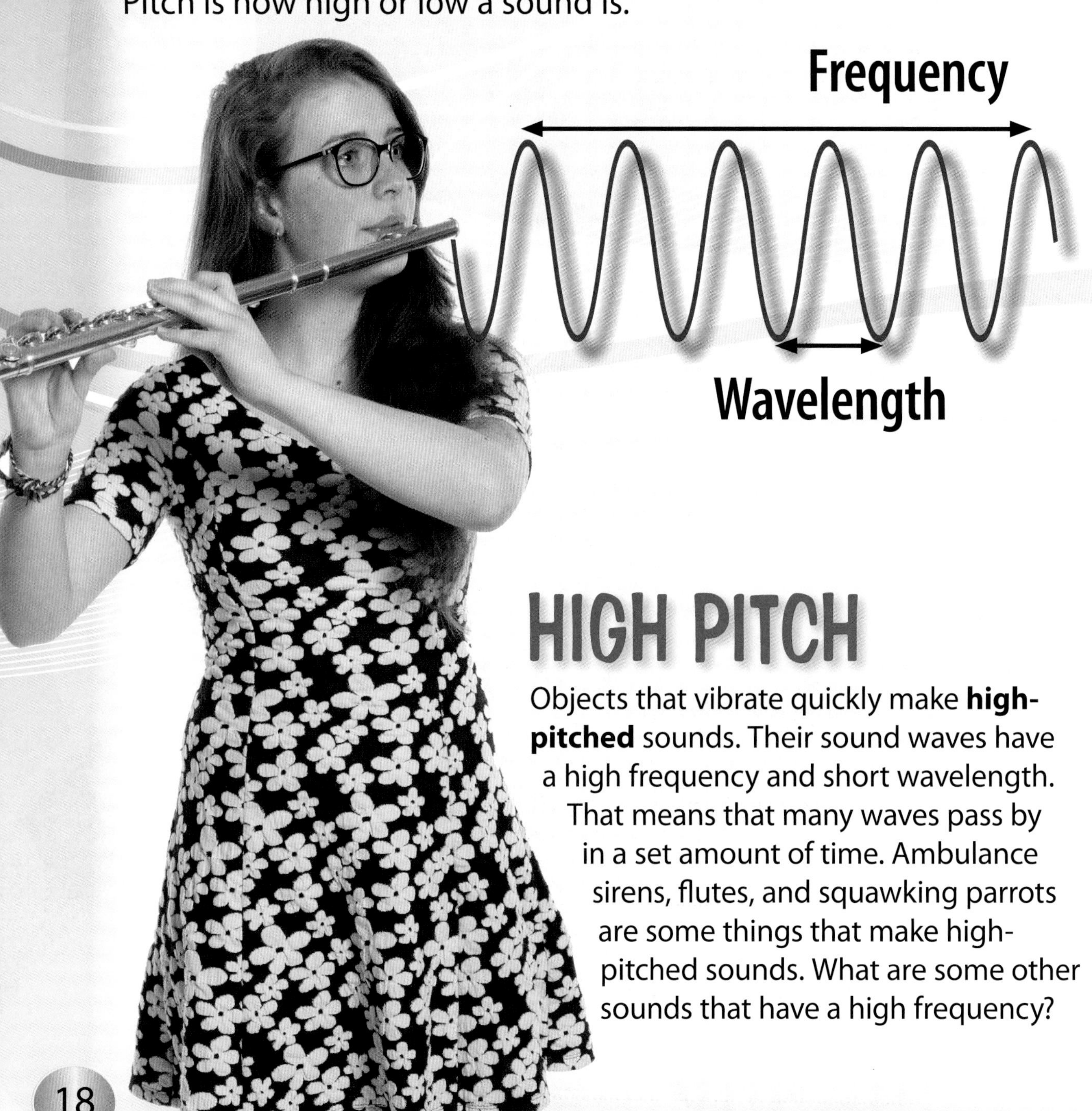

HIGH PITCH

Objects that vibrate quickly make **high-pitched** sounds. Their sound waves have a high frequency and short wavelength. That means that many waves pass by in a set amount of time. Ambulance sirens, flutes, and squawking parrots are some things that make high-pitched sounds. What are some other sounds that have a high frequency?

LOW PITCH

Objects that vibrate slowly make **low-pitched** sounds. Their sound waves have a low frequency and long wavelength. That means that few waves pass by in a set amount of time. Rumbling trucks, tubas, and growling dogs make low-pitched sounds. What other sounds have a low frequency?

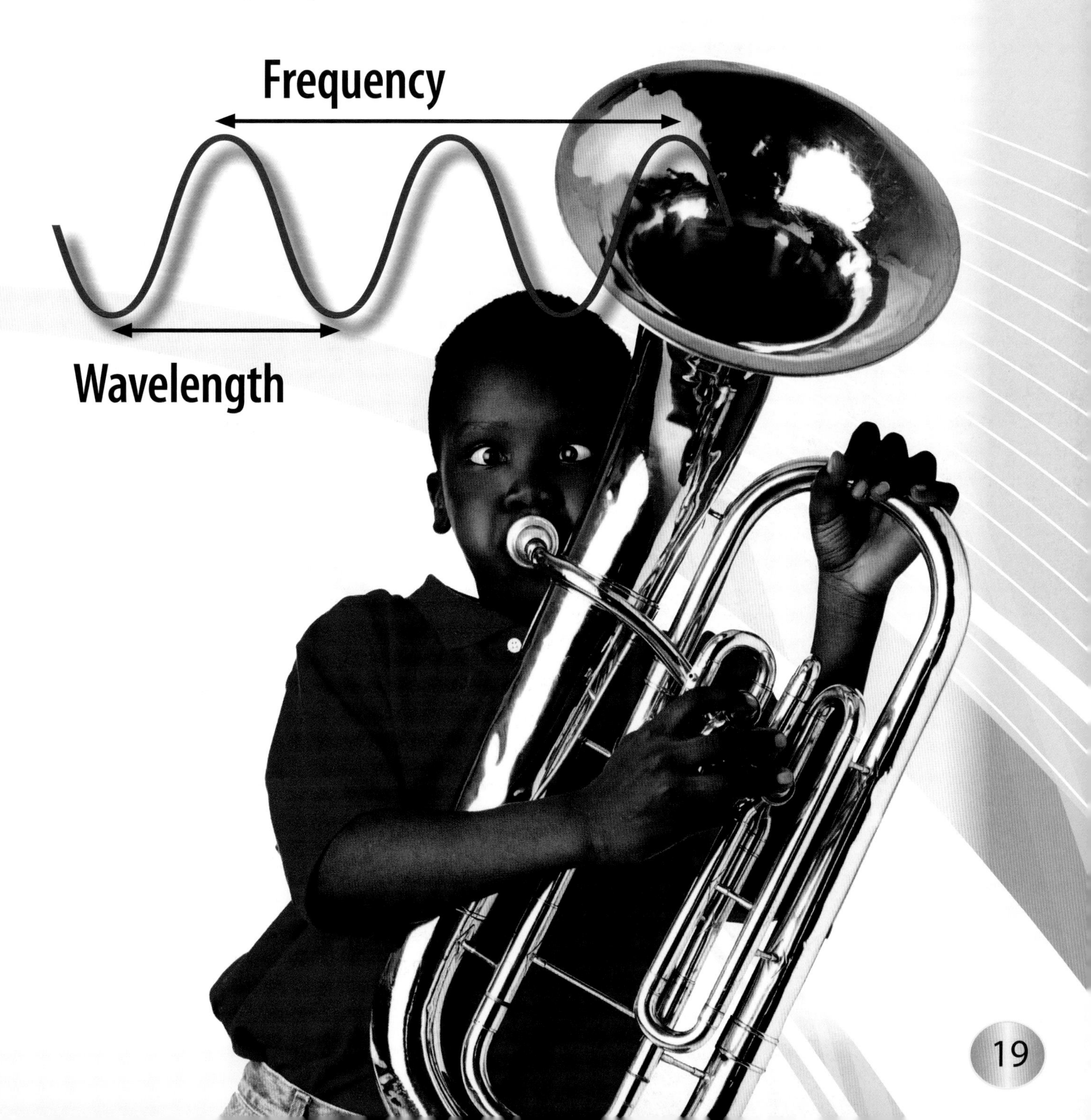

FULL VOLUME

The amplitude of a sound wave tells us how much energy the wave has. If a sound wave has a high amplitude, it has a lot of energy and is powerful. If a sound wave has a low amplitude, it has little energy and is weak. We hear the amplitude of a sound wave as the sound's **volume**. Volume is how loud or soft a sound is.

LOUD AND CLEAR

Some sounds are loud. A hammer pounding, a lion roaring, and a rocket launching are all sources of loud sounds. The sound waves that travel from these sources have high amplitudes and a lot of energy. These sounds have high volumes, so you can hear them clearly from far away.

SHAKE, RATTLE, and ROLL

Sounds that are very loud have big, powerful sound waves. They have a lot of energy and make strong vibrations that you can feel. If you touch a speaker while very loud music is playing, you will feel the speaker vibrating. If a noisy airplane flies over your home, you might feel the ground shake and hear your windows rattle.

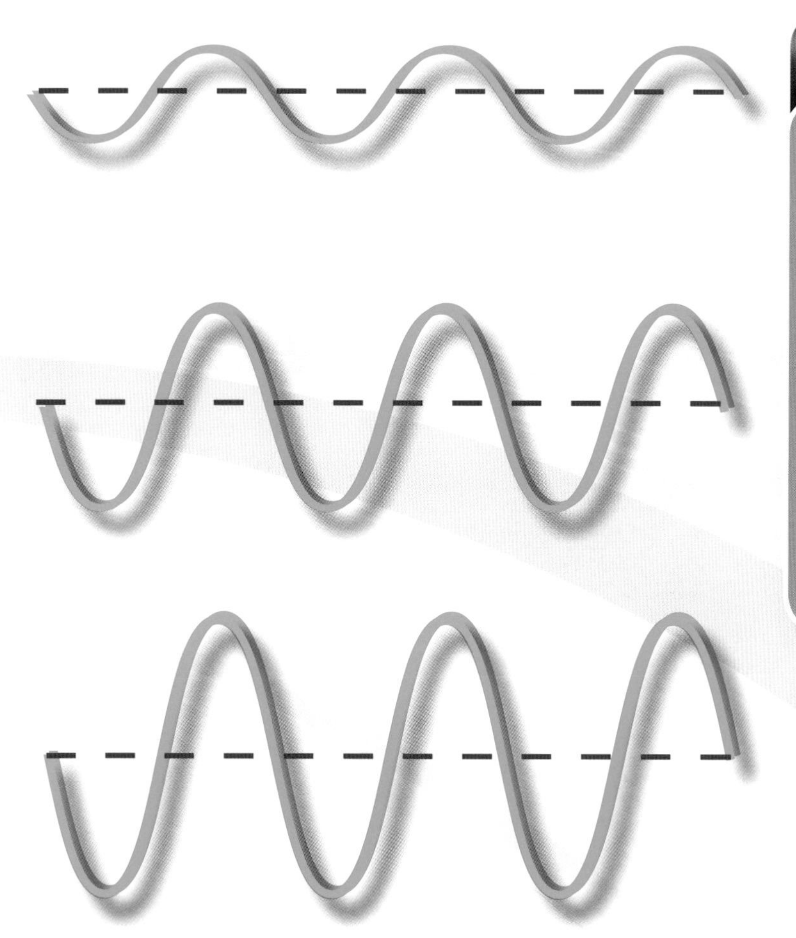

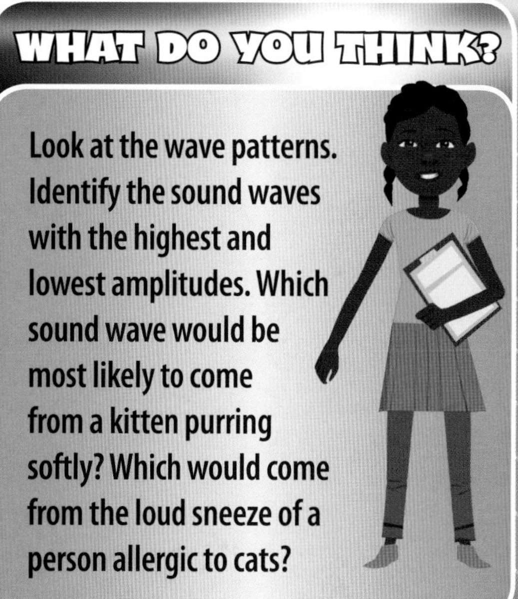

WHAT DO YOU THINK?

Look at the wave patterns. Identify the sound waves with the highest and lowest amplitudes. Which sound wave would be most likely to come from a kitten purring softly? Which would come from the loud sneeze of a person allergic to cats?

QUIET AS A MOUSE

Some sounds are soft. A whisper, a cat purring, and a pin dropping are all sources of soft sounds. Sound waves from these sources have low amplitudes and do not carry a lot of energy. These sounds have low volumes, so you can hear them only if you are nearby and listen carefully.

HEARING THINGS

You hear different sounds in different places. At home, you might hear soft sounds like a clock ticking, the refrigerator humming, or the bathroom tap drip-drip-dripping. You might hear high-pitched sounds like a closet door squeaking or your brother practicing his clarinet. There are all sorts of soft, loud, high, and low sounds all around. You just need to listen!

You probably make a loud sound when your favorite soccer team wins a game!

THINK OUT LOUD

The images on the following page show some sounds you might hear at school each day. Think about the volume of each of the sounds. Then put them in order from the loudest to the softest sounds. Which sound would have the highest amplitude? Which sound would have the lowest amplitude? Draw sound waves to **represent** the loudest and softest sounds.

PITCH IN

Look at the images showing the school sounds again. Now think about the pitch of each of the sounds. Rank them from the highest pitch to the lowest pitch. Which sound would have the highest frequency? Which sound would have the lowest frequency? Draw sound waves to represent these sounds.

Use this chart to help you draw the waves for your school sounds. Remember that louder sounds have greater amplitude. We show these sounds with higher waves. Sounds with higher pitch have higher frequencies. We show these sounds with shorter wavelengths.

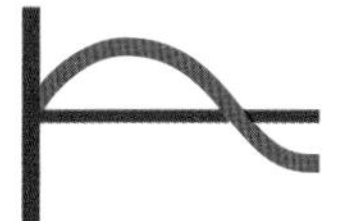

Lower pitch

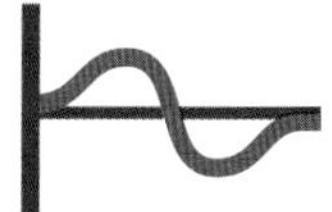

Quieter

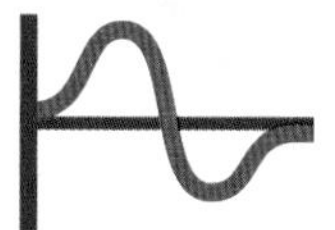

Louder

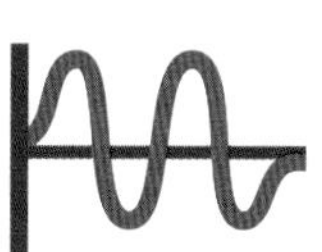

Higher pitch

MOVING THROUGH MATTER

You have heard all about the properties of sound waves. But did you know that these properties can change? Sound waves change when they move through different types of matter. Each type of matter is made up of a different number of molecules. Some types of matter have few molecules spread far apart. Other types of matter have many molecules packed closely together. We describe matter with many molecules as **dense**.

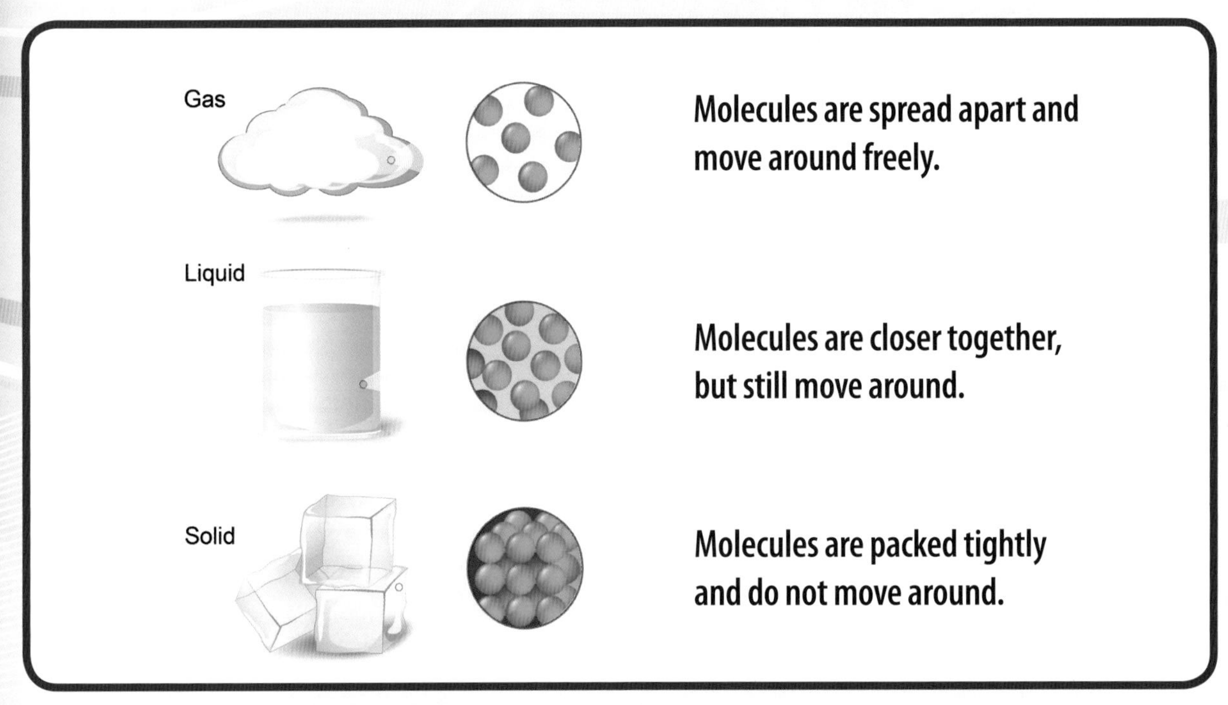

SOLID, LIQUID, and GAS

Solid objects, such as iron and steel, are very dense. They have many molecules packed closely together. Sound travels fast through solid objects because their molecules can pass sound energy to nearby molecules quickly. Water and other liquids are less dense and have fewer molecules than solids. The molecules are more spread out, so it takes more time for sound waves to reach them. Air and other gases are the least dense of all. They have fewer molecules and they are farther apart, so sound passes through this type of matter at a slower speed.

THE SPEED OF SOUND

The speed of sound waves affects how we hear different sounds. For example, when a sound wave travels quickly, it has a lot of energy and high amplitude. A sound wave with higher amplitude makes a louder sound. When a sound wave travels slowly, it has less energy and lower amplitude. A sound wave with lower amplitude makes a softer sound.

The speed of a sound wave is not the same as its frequency! Speed refers to how fast a wave passes through a certain point. Frequency refers to how often a wave passes a certain point.

Hear how sound travels through different types of matter by tapping your fingers on a solid surface, such as a door or your desk. Listen to the tapping sound that travels through air. Then put your ear against the surface and try it again. Which sounds louder? Explain why.

WHAT DO YOU THINK?

Imagine that you and a friend are at opposite ends of a long tunnel. A steel pipe runs along the length of the tunnel. If you banged on the pipe and yelled to your friend at the same time, which sound would your friend hear first? Explain your thinking.

HAVE YOU HEARD?

Our ears catch all sorts of sounds, but we cannot hear every type of sound. Some sounds have very low amplitude, so they are too soft for people to hear. Other sounds have a very high frequency. Humans cannot hear these high-pitched sounds. Dogs, cats, owls, elephants, and many other animals can hear sounds that humans cannot hear.

Which one of these cheering fans is not manipulating sound waves?

CHANGING SOUND WAVES

We can **manipulate** sound waves in order to hear a wider range of sounds. To manipulate means to use or change something for a certain purpose. We can make sound waves travel at different wavelengths, amplitudes, and frequencies. Changing sound waves can change the volume and pitch of sounds and make them **audible**, or able to be heard.

SHOUT IT OUT!

Have you ever cupped your hands around your mouth when you were shouting to a friend? That is a simple way to manipulate sound. Normally, sound waves travel out from a source in all directions. If you yell to a friend, the sound waves are scattered all around you. When you cup your hands around your mouth, you direct the sound waves where you want them to go. More sound energy reaches your friend and your message comes across loud and clear.

A megaphone is a cone-shaped device that amplifies sound waves and aims them in a certain direction.

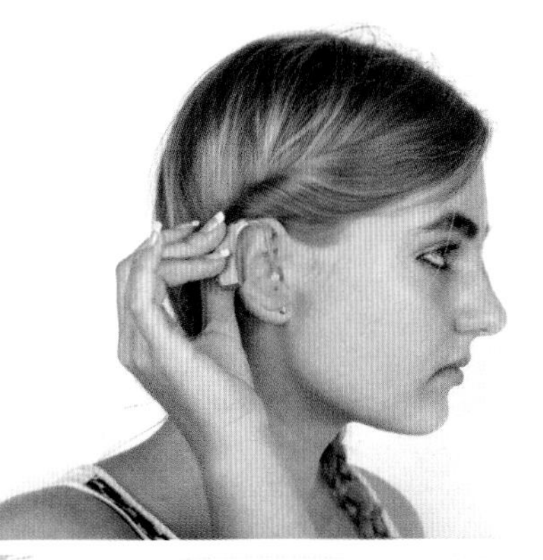

A person who does not hear well may use a hearing aid. A hearing aid is a small device that fits inside or behind the ear and makes sounds louder for the person using it.

SOUND MACHINES

We use different devices to manipulate sound waves in different ways. We use **synthesizers** in music to change the pitch and volume of sounds. A synthesizer is a tool that looks like a piano keyboard but can mimic sounds or create new ones. We use microphones and loudspeakers so large groups of people can hear us talking or singing. These devices **amplify** sound, or make it louder.

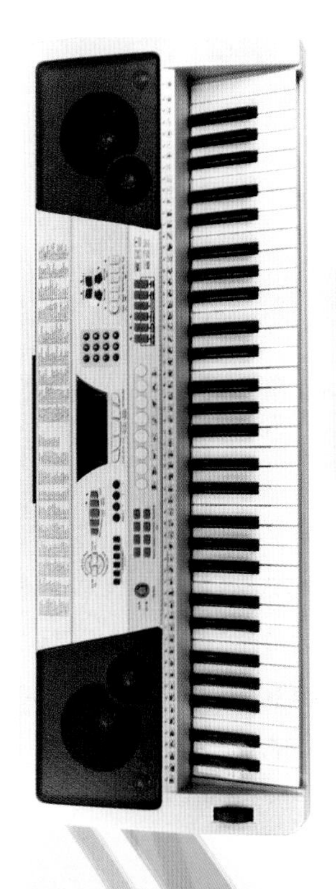

YOU CAN'T BEAT AN EARDRUM

You and your friends can make a **model** eardrum to see how you hear. A model is a representation of a real object. It helps you understand things that are very small, big, complex, or difficult to see—such as eardrums, found deep inside your ears. Making this model will show you how different sound waves make your eardrums vibrate in different ways. Your brain interprets those vibrations as different sounds.

What You Need

- a large bowl with a wide opening
- plastic wrap
- a large elastic band (optional)
- 20–30 grains of uncooked rice
- pots and pans, musical instruments, or any other objects that can be used to make sound
- a pencil and notebook

What to Do

Step 1

Stretch plastic wrap tightly over the opening of the bowl. Make sure there are no gaps around the edges. You can put a large elastic band around the rim of the bowl to help keep the plastic wrap tight. The plastic wrap represents the thin material that makes up your eardrum.

Step 2

Place the grains of rice on top of the plastic wrap.

Step 3

Now it is time to make some noise! Get close to the model eardrum. Bang your pots and pans or toot your horn. The rice will jump and dance around. The movement of the rice shows that the plastic wrap is vibrating. That is the same thing that happens when your eardrums receive sound waves—except you do not have rice in your ears!

Step 4

Write down your **observations** in your notebook. Observations are all the things you notice by listening and watching carefully. What is the volume and pitch of the sound? Does the rice move quickly or slowly? Does the rice jump a lot or hardly at all?

Step 5

Manipulate the sounds and observe what happens to the rice. Change the amplitude of the sound waves by banging the pots louder or softer. Change the frequency of the sound waves by playing a different **note** on the musical instrument. How else could you manipulate the sound waves before they reach your model eardrum? Get creative and drum up some great ideas!

MAKE SOME WAVES!

Use the observations in your notebook to make some waves. Draw a diagram that represents the sound waves you made the first time you used your model eardrum. Label the amplitude, wavelength, and frequency of the sound wave. Then draw a diagram that shows how the sound waves looked when you changed the source, volume, or pitch of the sound.

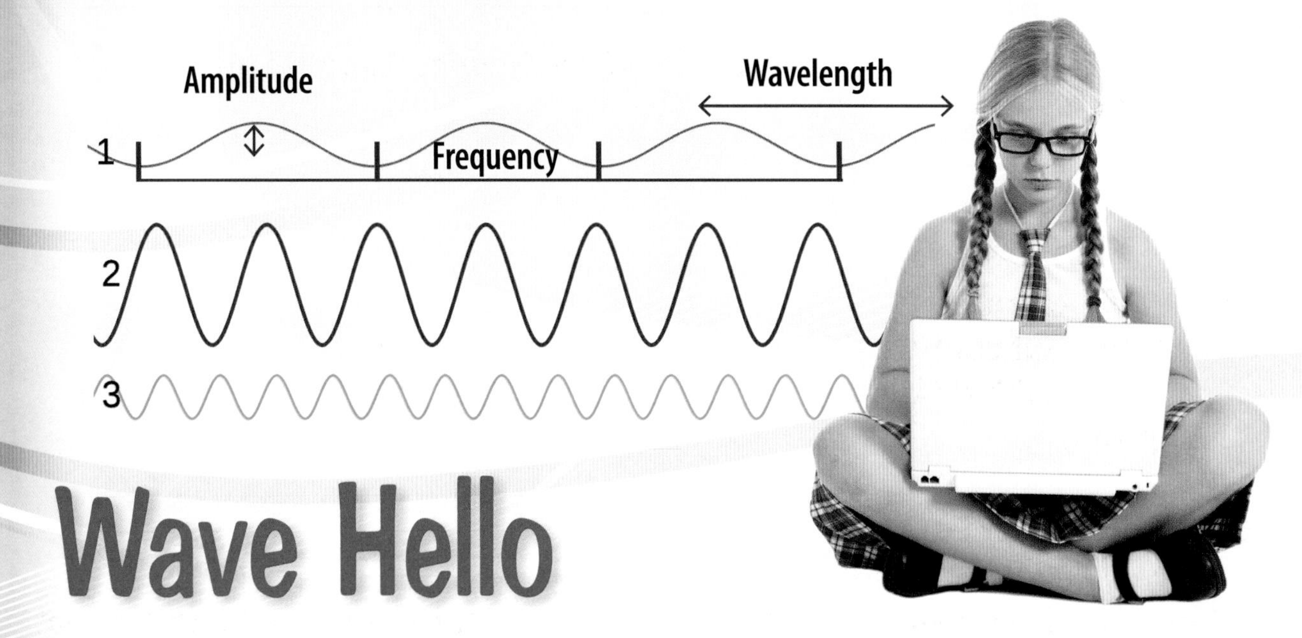

Wave Hello

Wave hello to other groups of students and then compare your work with theirs. How are your models and diagrams the same? How are they different? Notice how the groups used different sources of sound and manipulated sound waves in different ways. Then work together to share your sound ideas and make some new waves.

Learning More

Solway, Andrew. *From Crashing Waves to Music Download: An Energy Journey Through the World of Sound*. Heinemann, 2015.

Wacholtz, Anthony. *Mummies and Sound*. Capstone Press, 2013.

Winterberg, Jenna. *Sound Waves and Communication*. Teacher Created Materials, 2015.

Woodford, Chris. *Experiments with Sound and Hearing*. Gareth Stevens Publishing, 2010.

Websites

DK Find Out: Sound
www.dkfindout.com/uk/science/sound/
Hear sounds with different properties and take a sensational sound quiz at this website.

KidsHealth: Your Ears
http://kidshealth.org/en/kids/ears.html#
Listen up and learn all about ears, loud music, health—and even earwax!—at this website.

For fun wave challenges, activities, and more, enter the code at the Crabtree Plus website below.

www.crabtreeplus.com/waves

Your code is:
caw17

Glossary

Some **boldfaced** words are defined where they appear in text.

cochlea A snail-shaped tube in the inner ear lined with hairs that vibrate and send signals to the brain
ear canal The tube that carries sound to the ear
eardrum Part of the ear that vibrates and moves tiny bones inside the ear
gas A form or state of matter that is invisible
high-pitched Making a high sound
interpret To understand the meaning behind an action, mood, or behavior
low-pitched Making a low sound
note A musical sound with a certain pitch
ossicles Tiny bones in the middle ear that vibrate and move sound to the inner ear
represent To use pictures, models, or other forms to take the place of something or show an idea
sound wave Something that carries sound vibrations from place to place
source Something that produces a vibration
synthesizer A tool that can mimic or create sounds
vibration A fast movement back and forth
vocal cords Thin parts in your throat that help you make sounds with your voice

Index